Echoes and Aftershocks
Vivian Kearney

ISBN-13: 978-1-63065-107-7
ISBN-10: 1-63065-107-9

PUKIYARI PUBLISHERS
www.pukiyari.com

Dedicated to my amazingly understanding husband,
Milo, our beloved children, Kathleen
and Sean, and awesome grandchildren, Ben, Eli,
Jeremy, Ian and Collin and our surviving
generation of families.
In memory of our missed relatives who were
murdered in the Holocaust and all victims of
cruelty and violence.

Thank you to Ani Palacios McBride for her patient
editing, to Judy Lackritz, Ellen
Ollervidez and Matthew Faulkner for welcoming,
encouraging and facilitating the
presentation of this second collection of my Holocaust
poems as they did for my
first collection about the Holocaust:
The Unfathomable - Holocaust and After.

Vivian

Table of Contents

Bontsche the Silent
(After the short story _Bontsche Schweig_ by I. L. Peretz)

Bontsche Schweig,
The silent one
Whose name fitted
Like a glove

Who lived a victim
Who died, was celebrated
In heaven
For his patient humility

And there was offered
Anything he wanted
As a recompense
For his horrendous earthly
Suffering

Who meekly asked
The celestial angels
For a hot roll with butter
Making them cry

Bontsche Schweig
Cruelly mistreated, unhelped –
A precursor
Of the unimaginable
Genocide

Another Forecaster

Trials, labyrinths, dehumanization
Turning the wrongly accused
Into easily disposed of vermin,

Trails leading nowhere

Kafka, what did you fear the most
From a blinding and blinded
Cruel bureaucracy ruling from
Fascism's grim castle

Vivian Kearney

Already There – Warnings Versus Hope

Hope sometimes
Is wrongly advised
Like preparing the usual breakfast
In the normal, comfortable way
Dismissing warnings as lies

Ich und Du
(After <u>I and Thou</u> by Martin Buber)

I and you – *ich und du*
When and why
Did we change to
I and it – *ich und das*

And fall into anger
And holocaust

Vivian Kearney

Get Ready

Suitcases, they told us
To pack suitcases with
The most needed stuff

What to take? What to leave?

Yes, we can be ready
With our necessities
We must

Onto the trains, then into the bunkers
At least we still have some home basics

Leave them now…
Your clothes, your shoes
Your hair, your glasses
That you used before
For your just passed life

Guess what
You won't even need
Your bodies

Your souls will fly free
Above the gas

Ghost Trains

The locked cattle car
Of a grim train
That no one knew
That everyone knew
Was really a horizontal elevator
To death chambers

Vivian Kearney

Political Boxes

FDR, a generally
Good president,
You prayed too
Why not for the persecuted Jews
Who begged for asylum
For some of politics' crumbs
During World War II

I Dreamed of a Child

I dreamed of
A child
Maybe three or five
All dressed
In a sparkling coat or tunic
Of a multicolored pattern
And careful embroidery

Who walked
(Or was led)
Into the night
And became a star
And never came back

Ich Hob Gechulemt Veign a Kind

Ich hob gechulemt veign
A kind
Efsher drei oder finf
Gekleidt
In a glantzndik
Oysegneintn mantl
In farsheedene koleern

Vivian Kearney

Gegangen alein
(Oder gefeert gevorn)
In di nacht arein
Un iz gevorn a shtern
Un iz keinmol nisht
Tzurikgekimen

Picture Children
(San Antonio Holocaust Museum's photograph of child victims just before being shot)

Fifteen little children
Stand facing the camera
One toddler girl cried
Tragedy loomed, she just knew
Some of the boys smiled, confused

None of their sweet faces
Stopped the guns
Or the people behind them

Vivian Kearney

Looking at Us

Do they look at us
From above's tender skies
Recalling their dreams
Of future descendants
They could have,
Should have loved

Today's children
Discussing the slaughter
Of their ancestors
Then able to return
To comfortable houses

To the warmth, the care
Of another era
Slowly birthed
On this shuddering earth

Should We Know How?

Do you want me to know
How you died
The exact details
Of how you were led
To the killing camp
The gas chamber
Where you were murdered

My aunt,
One daughter survivor,
Like probably many
Didn't want to be told
The unbearable
Particulars

If I would research
What you suffered
From readings,
Explicit descriptions,
Movies

Would it honor or embarrass you
And those who outlived your death

Who had talked with you,
Worked with you
Who knew you
As capable, loveable persons
Not Nazi-threatening vermin
Tricked into atrocious deaths

Beyond Words

The shoes
The mounds
Of those abandoned shoes

Left outside
The crematoria
Can you fill them
With your mourning,
Remembering soul

To reconstitute
Their departed spirits

Then you might walk
Their last steps

And hear
Their horrified cries
Beyond words

Vivian Kearney

Objects as Mourners

The soft blue baby shoe
Scuffed and pummeled
Left behind
Before the gas took its owner

Allows generations later
To understand much more
What happened to people
Families, fellow humans
Before

Speak, sad shoes, tell us
How with high hopes
You were fashioned
How your happy usefulness
Your excited first steps
Were cut off
So wildly

And you acquired
A longer-lived
Mourner's mission

Photographs

We look at the formal, serious faces
In those enduring photographs
And grieve ever again that

Little did they know
They had only four more years to live
Seven with luck and stamina

Their time burned up eventually
We don't know exactly
Where or when

Unless they and their tattooed numbers
Were documented
As some were
Ever so systematically

By some perpetrators
Of that cleansing project

Vivian Kearney

Recovered Present

O thank you for
My beautiful red plaid
Covered present

This wonderful journal
White for the blank pages
I will soon fill
Red for the fun times recorded
And the plaid lines for organizing
All sorts of thoughts and observations
To practice my beginnings
As a writer, maybe a reporter

I didn't know
The red would be
For so much blood shed
Without reason
White for innocence
Plaid for the rest
Of my short life
Behind bars
Of hatred

Dear Diarist

My dearest Anne
Don't worry, don't fear
You haven't disappeared

Though
Tragically stopped
When you were led away

Your diary
Detailing days
Of so much suffering
In hiding
Has made you
A forever journalist

You are brought
To virtual life
Every time
Your story, our history
Is read, retold

Your soul continues
To walk with us
Along our roads

Vivian Kearney

Left Behind

Cherished, though humble
Or silver-lovely
Some objects
Members of a family
Had parked and buried
With what heart-pounding hopes
For retrieval

Later, much later
Discovered by strangers
With dark questions

Why and how
Did these survive
And not their
Protective,
Unprotected
Owners
And their lost
Biographies

Internet News from Auschwitz

Artifacts continue to surface
Each surviving object
A toy, a bowl,
A comb, a button
A death camp uniform

A testimony, evidence
Of its owners'
Assassination by racial
Prejudice

May these tragic finds
Keep admonishing us
To honor our once
Families, neighbors

And try
To help keep
Present souls
Bodies and belongings
Happily, thankfully,
Together

Wielke Oczy

The tag taken off
The to-be-recycled ringbinder –
Wielke Oczy –

Little Polish
Long-ago *shtetl*
Dear old village
Of family legends

Sticks to my hand
And won't
Let
Go

Objects Become

Our present
Objects sometimes
Seem to become
Our lost relative, homes

Our present
Objects can become
Needle and thread
Stitching a quilted
New life
With colorful scraps
And some blank patches
Of forgotten or unspoken
Memories

Our present
Objects have somehow become
Symbols of survival, trying
To rescue us, help us escape
From a long ago
Volcanic pit

The distant, fearsome hole
Of the still unfathomable
Holocaust

Vivian Kearney

Echoes

This painful echo
This nostalgia for
What should have been

Wants to speak
Of a heart search
For our murdered family
And cry silent tears
With the survivors

Clinging Cinders

Cinderella, will you clean
The ashes from your hands
Fingernails and

Take the extra charcoal
To use as lead
For drawing, writing
With blackened tears

Please do

For the perished ones
Who went up in flames
In Europe and all over
This gassed planet

Vivian Kearney

Research

Search, I keep searching
The library
Lackadaisically

Once I did see the name
Of the orphanage where I was hidden
Where maybe my molecules
Are still pining

But the reference
Turns around corners, down alleys
Of the holocaust shelf books
Charging me to look longer

For who was the man
Who founded the safe haven
Was that in the 17th century?

There, almost there
In the B indices – *Dom Bodouina*

Wait, perhaps I'm tracking
The wrong spelling

Search, why all this research
Now and long ago
As I went rifling
Into closets, drawers
House of my rescuing,
First generation family

What did I hope to find
So fearfully?

The answers are still
Out of reach
For who knows what questions
Puzzle completion
Revelations

Identify

Say the names
See the faces
Hear the cries
And pause and mourn
In front of nullifying hate

Lost, Gone

Although when
I include the names of
Disappeared relatives
In a daily prayer list

Holding a continuous *shiva* service
Of sorts

It's always a shock
To realize
That so many first names
Of the Rossiners, Kundorfs
Kantorovitches, Engelsbergs
Hoffmans

Are lost to us, absent
From our collective memories
Ever evident lacunae
In the biographies
Of the after generations
Just able to find mourning refuge
In generalizations

We can't even say
Specific *kaddish*
For their individual souls

Their identities
Irretrievable as clouds
Intangible as smoke
Escaped, unresearchable

Gone

Brethren

Yet you dear brethren
Who were in ground zero
Of the Holocaust

Whose names we may not know
You aren't too heavy
To carry around

God willing, as long as we live
We'll keep your ashes
In our memory jars

God helping
For many millennia
Of later generations

God granting
Prayers for peace
For no more
Such memorials

Vivian Kearney

And We Can

And we can
Rely on the tailoring capacities
Of remaining memory

Pin its special moments
Shapes and patterns
Sew, fit and hem them
To just the right size and length

O family of seamstresses
Carpenters, leather workers
Printers and tailors
Where did you write and sew your war memories
Into what secretive pockets
To create new lives, in brighter colors
For your children's normalized clothes
And unburdened spirits

Answers Out of Reach

Explanations have been
Buried
Out of reach

With now
Silent families in
Mass graves

Which is where
They, the real witnesses
The clarifying victims
Were sent
Too early, too soon

So, there seems to be
A decided pull
To give a parallel burial

To the possibilities
Of our near survivors
Completely answering
Our unspoken
Orphaned questions

Vivian Kearney

Over

Over, now evaporated
The oft get-togethers

That we celebrated
With the escaped crowd

That is now quite dispersed
Was it my fault, our fault?

Gone the warmth of a neurotic group
Survival has been overcome

Gone the language of a million ironies
And we didn't even say goodbye

Should old societies be forgot
Or be brought into nostalgia's searchlight?

Let's walk beyond our survivor guilt
Into forgiving lands with *mitzvot* bright

Ich und Du – To Freda

Running out of the holocaust
Mother and baby in arms
Grey metal
Statue larger than life size
In Montreal's Jewish Public Library

Forever escaping
Forever holding

Though she really
Did run quickly
Did hold me
So carefully
For so long

Until she could
Until she had to
Let go
And leave this world

And I lost
Her lullaby song

Two Survivor Brothers – Sholem and Yitzchak

One secular brother wanted to study war
His father and family asked what for
Soldiering was not our interest before
It's not part of our peace-yearning lore

The other brother stood fast in faith
And tradition. Both had the fate
To survive beyond hell's implacable hate
Though for so many such luck came too late

These siblings' hows and whys
Sent to contrasting skies

Run, Run, Memory

Run, run, memory
Nostalgically
In leaf-blown streets
After figures in black gabardines

With *shtreimelech, yamulkes*
Payes and *talitim*
Down Bloomfield street
In Montreal's *shtetele*-replacing
Orthodox Jewish community

To ask and hear
Whence comes your ability
To worship God,
To follow tradition

Even after pogroms
Exiles and the Holocaust

How do you find the grace
To keep praising *Adonai*
And through it all
Celebrate His gifts of religious life

Vivian Kearney

Their Bags and Mine

Bags I keep carrying
For my subbing job
Or whenever, wherever
Why

With readied supplies
Books, notebooks,
Sweater, umbrella
Pens and pencils
Why

Maybe in remembrance
Of the suitcases,
Bags and clothes they carried
We can see
In those seventy-some-year-old photos
Why

Shlepped to the *umschlagplatz*
For the forced train rides
Then thrown away, un-needed
Why

No real answer

When they arrived
With more desperate questions
At the set-up
End-destination

Living With PTSD

Wake up, don't sleep, don't follow that route
You're not rushing enough – I have to shout
I still hear there will be another horrible
Action – keep calm and collected but get out

Should the woods be run to or from
Every tree can sing of peace, although
Behind each bush can lurk ferocious enemies
We don't have safety, sympathy or home

Desperate commands years later, lovingly meant
To assure your health, insisting on details
That may seem unimportant but could be
Dangerous mistakes, people's undoing

Traumatic syndrome, worries ongoing
Through generations inheriting the wounds
Should fearful critics then be criticized for
Hair trigger nerves and dramatic warnings?

Vivian Kearney

Why Don't You Speak, Memory?

Guarded
Memory

Repressed
Concealed

Distorted
Constrained

Or stonewalled
True to the grave
Of not sharing

Quelling the Problematic Question

I love you, o survivor family of mine
Whatever you did during the war
To stay alive, to help others

As much as you could, through
Harrowing escapes and battles
During the horrendous *Shoah*

And you certainly saved me
To be here, to be grateful
For enlisting me, mentoring me
In life's never-ending school

Vivian Kearney

If Asked

Why did you survive
Out of all those
Sweet children, good families
Persecuted, victimized
Unhelped people

Each with their hopes
Of a happy, long life
Before brutal plans
Starved and killed so many

If I answer it was luck, a lottery
As Sholem declared
Then God is freed from
Accusations of unfairness
But, unfortunately, fortune is given
The crown of power
While questions are still not answered

Freda believed
You must do everything to stay alive
And push away the death wish
Others wanted for you

However you can't say
The persecuted were being punished
For carelessness, or lack of clever wills

Definitely, I can't claim
(I was an infant)
It was my wise survival skills
Rather heroic rescuers' efforts and kindness

Then can this existential debate
Ever be refereed or won?...

We can only honor the victims
Not with impossible questions

But with prayers that their eternal souls
Are happily living forever
In God's glorious heaven

It Hurts

Insomnia images
Of victims reaching
Into the night
It hurts, Lord

When I try
To tear at
The scab of indifference
It hurts, Lord

Although
Letting ghosts
Weep again
It hurts, Lord

Their little *shtetls*
Belonging to us as well
Burned and gassed
Why such evil, Lord

Uncovering
Discovering
Unforgettable chasms

In our DNA,
In history's shadows
It hurts, Lord

Shared Quandaries

So… like me
Others felt it too
Suffer it now
The accusing sinkhole
Of survivor confusion

Asking why in the world
Didn't you, don't you
Ask vital questions
Do more family research
Feel more of their pain

Dedicate yourself
To the specific lives
Of the six million

Why did you let
Your life get in the way

And let the victims become
Object stones of memory
On graves of forgetting

Instead of re-membering
Those undone persons

To find some redemptions
From survivor guilt
Of the second, third
And later generations

May We All Be

Willing to hear the candle burning
Willing to see the bells tolling
Willing to be haunted by ghosts

Willing to pick up shards of prayer
And walk with wounded hearts
Willing to build sanctuary cities of care

For descendants and ancestors
For neighbors near and far
For we are all bound spiritually

And should, humanistically
Sorrows and sunshine share

Aftershocks

Holocaust and
Aftershocks
As the country beneath their feet
Quaked and imploded
With more dangers and horrors

And now as a survivor
And child of a survivor
I'm still reeling
With second-hand PTSD, OCD
And find it difficult
To dream calmly

But it's past
What about the present
Fear for others
Another child
Might pass away
In torment

Unless pleas are heard
And prayers are granted
For an end to suffering
Now

Lessons Learned

Don't hate, don't shun and let
Your heart live peacefully, though aware
Take care of your mind and soul
Keep them civilized, kind and progressive

For the wrong trains once prepared
To roll out of civilization can move
Faster, heavier
Than can be stopped
Once started

Vivian Kearney

Working Empathy

Who will cry with the betrayed ones?
With *La Llorona* – the weeping woman
For her drowned children
In *Nueva España*

Who will shout?
Es brent, unzer kleiner shtetl brent!
It's burning, our little village is burning
With the pogrommed Jews

O to realize
And empathize
With all the world's tragedies
In every language

O to be part of
To work for
Somehow
The rescue

Angelic *Mentschn*

Angels among us
To the left, to the right
Offering a barn, a room
Some soup, an open door
A bouquet, friendship

Mentschn, good Samaritans
Commissioned to carry
God's saving light

Vivian Kearney

Don't Let Down Your Hands

Was Freda's mantra
And maybe
That's just how
I was saved
From the war

Because somebody,
Some people, by turns
Said
Let her be,
She can be
Rescued

Thus may
This child,
Other children prove

Life goes on
By Heaven renewed

Not on the Last Road

With the Yiddish song
That the *partisans* had proclaimed
Under leaden clouds

"Zog nisht keynmol
az du geyst dem letstn veg
ven himlen blayene
farshteln bloye teg"

Never say
You are going down
The last road
That the skies
Won't ever be blue
Again

Spiritually
Don't stop walking

And don't let
Down your hands
Or theirs

Vivian Kearney

Surrendering Survivor Guilt

Who will forgive survival
When victims have passed away
To whom and where do we look
When past skies were cruel and gray

Let us now walk to numinous places
With songs of hope and prayers
Leaving existential answers
To the Father we all share

Heritage

The insights that fell upon
Me while still living on earth
Before being victimized
By murder, death

I give to you
The words, laughter,
Surprises and smiles
Wry and otherwise

I send on the breeze
And love's tender ties
Now you are the poem
Continuing my being